To James
from Granny
1998

G000067188

The Promised Child

Told by Carine Mackenzie
Illustrations by Fred Apps

Published by Christian Focus
Geanies House, Tain, Ross-shire, IV20 1TW, Scotland
© 1997 Christian Focus Publications
Printed in Singapore

Jesus, the Son of God, was born into this world in a wonderful way. His mother Mary was a poor, young woman. She lived in the village of Nazareth in the land of Israel.

One day, an angel came to Mary and gave her an amazing piece of news.

'You are going to have a baby boy. You will call his name Jesus.'

'How can that be?' she asked.

'The baby is the Son of God. You will have this child by the special power of the Holy Spirit.'

Mary was engaged to be married to Joseph. When he heard that Mary was expecting a baby, he was very alarmed and unhappy. God sent Joseph a message in a dream.

He heard an angel say, 'Do not be afraid to take Mary as your wife. The child that she is expecting is the Son of God. When the baby boy is born, you shall call his name Jesus (which means Saviour) for he shall save his people from their sins.'

So Joseph was happy to marry Mary.

A special order came from the Roman ruler, Caesar Augustus, that everyone in the empire had to go back to their home town to be enrolled. Joseph's family came from Bethlehem so that meant that he and Mary had to travel from Nazareth to Bethlehem. Mary's baby was due to be born very soon but she still had to make the journey.

When they reached Bethlehem the whole town was busy. They could find no room at the inn. They had to find shelter where the animals were fed.

When the baby boy was born, Mary wrapped him up carefully and laid him in the manger for a cot. A manger was normally used for holding straw and food that the sheep would eat. That made a bed for baby Jesus.

In the country-side nearby, shepherds were out that night as usual watching over their sheep. Suddenly an angel appeared to them and the bright shining light of the glory of the Lord dazzled them. They were afraid.

'Don't be afraid,' the angel said. 'I bring good news for you and all the people. Today a Saviour has been born in Bethlehem. He is Christ the Lord. If you go now you will find the baby in a manger.'

Suddenly there was a crowd of angels, each praising God, saying, 'Glory to God in the highest. Peace and good will to all people.'

When the angels had gone back to heaven, the shepherds turned to one another and said, 'Let's go to Bethlehem and see for ourselves what the Lord has told us about.'

They hurried to Bethlehem and found Mary and Joseph, and the baby lying in the manger.

The shepherds passed on the good news to everyone they met. They praised and worshipped God as they went back to their work.

When the baby was eight days old he was given the name JESUS, just as the angel had told Joseph and Mary. Mary and Joseph took the young baby Jesus to the temple to present him to the Lord and to offer a sacrifice as the law of God required.

In the temple at Jerusalem they met a man called Simeon. Simeon was a holy man who loved the Lord. God had given him a special promise - he would not die until he had actually seen Christ, the promised Saviour.

When Mary and Joseph brought Jesus that day into the temple, Simeon took the baby in his arms. He knew that God's promise to him had now come to pass.

'I am ready to die,' he said, 'for I have seen God's salvation.' Mary and Joseph were amazed at what Simeon said. Simeon blessed them.

An old lady called Anna then saw baby Jesus. Anna was a widow who lived in the temple and prayed all day long, and at night too. She too gave thanks to God when she met the special baby, Jesus.

She passed on the good news of Jesus to all the people that she met who were wondering about God's plan to provide a Saviour.

Wise men from the East came to look for Jesus. They had seen a special star in the sky, which prompted them to look in Jerusalem for the King of the Jews. King Herod was troubled when he heard their story.

'Find out more about this King of the Jews. Where would he be born?' he asked his religious leaders.

'The Scriptures tell us that he would be born in Bethlehem,' they told him.

He sent the wise men to Bethlehem saying, 'Look for the young child there and come and tell me when you have found him.'

When they left King Herod, the wise men were guided by a special star, right to the house where Jesus was. The wise men were delighted. They came into the house and fell down before the young child Jesus and worshipped him.

They realised that he was the Son of God. They gave him lovely presents of gold, frankincense and myrrh.

When they left the house, they did not go back to tell Herod where Jesus was, for God had warned them in a dream. They went back home another way.

The angel of the Lord then spoke to Joseph in a dream.

'Take young Jesus and Mary away from here. Go to Egypt. Stay there until I tell you it is safe to return. King Herod wants to destroy the young child.'

So Joseph, Mary and Jesus left under cover of darkness and travelled to the land of Egypt.

After Herod died, the angel spoke to Joseph in another dream.

'Take the young child and his mother back to Israel. The ones who wanted to kill him are dead. It is safe to go back.'

Joseph took the little family back to Israel and they settled in the village of Nazareth.

Jesus grew up there - he was a wise and good boy who lived in a way that was pleasing to God, his Heavenly Father.

We should remember every day of the year the wonderful fact that Jesus was born. The angels told shepherds that the new-born baby was the Saviour of the world - this good news was for all people - you as well.

God sent his Son to the world to be the Saviour because he loves us so much. Our response should be to believe in the Saviour and to obey his word.